NATIONAL
GEOGRAPH

Mighty Machines

Kate McGough

Mighty machines are used to make tall buildings. The machines are built to do different things.

2

3

This machine is a **bulldozer**.
It pushes away rocks and dirt.
It clears the building site.

5

This machine is a **front-end loader**.
It scoops up rocks and dirt.

7

This machine is a **dump truck**.
It carries rocks and dirt.
It dumps its load away
from the building site.

9

This machine is an **excavator**.
It digs into the dirt.
It makes big holes in the ground.

This machine is a **concrete mixer**.
It mixes concrete on the building site.
Concrete is used to build tall buildings.

This machine is a **tower crane**.
It lifts heavy loads into the air.
It helps build very tall buildings.

15

Mighty machines made these tall buildings.